No Nonsense Management

THE NO NONSENSE LIBRARY

NO NONSENSE CAREER GUIDES

Managing Time
No Nonsense Management
How to Choose a Career
How to Re-enter the Workforce
How to Write a Resume
No Nonsense Interviewing

NO NONSENSE FINANCIAL GUIDES

How to Use Credit and Credit Cards
Investing in Mutual Funds
Investing in the Stock Market
Investing in Tax Free Bonds
Understanding Money Market Funds
Understanding IRA's
Understanding Treasury Bills and Other U.S. Government Securities
Understanding Common Stocks
Understanding Stock Options and Futures Markets
Understanding Social Security
Understanding Insurance
How to Plan and Invest for Your Retirement
Making a Will and Creating Estate Plans
Understanding Condominiums and Co-ops
How to Buy a Home
Understanding Mortgages and Home Equity Loans

NO NONSENSE SUCCESS GUIDES

NO NONSENSE HEALTH GUIDES

NO NONSENSE COOKING GUIDES

NO NONSENSE PARENTING GUIDES

NO NONSENSE CAR GUIDES

NO NONSENSE CAREER GUIDE™

No Nonsense
Management

Andrew Ambraziejus

Longmeadow Press

Cover design by Nancy Sabato
Interior design by Richard Oriolo

ISBN: 0–681–41403–0

Printed in the United States of America

First Edition

0 9 8 7 6 5 4 3 2 1

Contents

Acknowledgements

The author would like to thank Irene Cibas Kong, Paul Fornario, John Gartner, David Reuther, Barbara Spence, Jane Venckus.

Introduction

Manage: "To handle or direct with a degree of skill or address . . . to treat with care . . . to exercise executive, administrative, and supervisory direction of . . . to alter by manipulation . . . to achieve one's purpose . . ."

The above are some of the definitions *Webster's* has given us for the word *manage*. There are various nuances to the word—various directions in which anyone who has been hired to manage other people can go. If you think about it, however, what it all comes down to is getting people to do what you think needs to be done. You use power, rewards, examples, praise, criticism, or any combination of these and other methods. If you use them well, you will be successful, freeing up time to do your own work, while feeling confident that your subordinates are doing theirs.

These definitions also remind us that to manage is to focus on people—not things or animals but creatures who are not always rational, who may be up one day and down the next, who may have their own ideas about how to do something. As recent experience has shown, the manager who remembers that he is dealing with people is the one who is going to be the most successful. It is a simple notion, but one all too often overlooked. The numbers on the bottom line or a high salary may be what you, as a manager, are going after, but it is the performance of the people who work for you that is going to get you there.

This basic recognition is not just a shift in popular thought or the latest business fad that will change with the next stock market crash. Most theories of management, based on research as well as on experience, have recognized the same thing. They have gone from advocating supposedly scientific working methods (where the knowledgeable boss tells the unquestioning subordinate what to do, and so on down the line) to more participatory ones (where the importance of working together and acknowledging everybody's value to an organization is recognized). This certainly doesn't mean that no one or everyone is in charge—the structure of the successful organization is still hierarchical. It is the way the people work within the structure that makes all the difference.

And that is the purpose of this book. *No Nonsense Management* discusses how you as manager can best work with those around you, motivating them to reach defined goals. Whether you have just been promoted to a supervisory position or have several departments reporting to you, remembering that people are key will stand you in good stead, no matter what task you will be trying to accomplish.

Part I

·····

WHAT IS A MANAGER?

1

...

Setting an Example: Self Inventory

This is a chapter of questions, questions that will help you examine what you think about your job, the people you work with, and most important, yourself. They do not provide answers. They are a way for you to come up with your own answers. Because there are so many situations and people involved, no one is going to give you easy, pat solutions to problems. The solutions will have to come from within yourself.

This is why self inventory is so important. It is a check on yourself and your job to make sure that the fit is right. You want to know what you enjoy or don't enjoy about the job so that you don't end up unconsciously taking out your frustrations on the position or on those you manage. It happens all too often: the brilliant, temperamental program manager who keeps hiring and firing assistants, always finding an excuse as to why they have failed him; the talented art director who produces stunning layouts, but is so protective of her work that her staff feels left out of the process; the distant, demanding vice president who runs his department by intimidation, while being very solicitous of other departments and colleagues. People begin to complain. Morale falls. There are attempts to solve the problem: meetings, discussions, new procedures are laid out. These solutions may work for a few weeks, but if underlying problems aren't acknowledged and addressed, then in the end nothing will change and the problems will continue.

The eight questions in this chapter are a guide to ascertaining the best place for yourself in the managerial world and will help you avoid the scenarios described above. They are a way to start out right, or to begin to correct anything that has gone wrong. Whether you are a newly promoted manager, a supervisor, or a higher-level officer, take a look at them and respond as honestly as you can.

Why are you in this job? It is amazing how many of us languish in unfulfilling jobs, not because we have to, but because we simply haven't carefully thought out what our possibilities are. After making an initial career choice, we've forgotten how to ask questions to keep ourselves motivated and fresh. Not being able to see this, we blame the job or those who work for us, finding fault where there is none. Asking yourself why you are in a particular job is not only a way of taking responsibility for yourself, but it starts the mind working on other possibilities that may open up to you.

Whether you are applying for a new job or reevaluating the one you are in, ask yourself the questions below and see what thoughts they bring forth. If you are happy with the answers, that's a good sign. If not, you should start thinking about making some changes.

- Are you in the job primarily for the money? Or does the job fill a more creative need?

- Does the job represent security and stability, which are important to you at this point in your life?
- Are you doing this job for your parents or someone else whose opinion you've always valued, possibly more than your own?
- Do you think you will get any moral gain from doing this job? Or does it simply provide you with something to do?
- Are you hiding from something, perhaps from an unhappy life at home, and this job is a good place in which to hide?
- Is this job temporary, a good jumping-off point for greener pastures? If it is, how long do you intend to stay there?
- Do you feel that the company is lucky to have you, or are you lucky to have the company? Why?
- What qualities does the job bring out in you?

What are your personality traits—both positive and negative? Cataloging your personal strengths and weaknesses— a *conscious* acknowledgment that you have both—will not only steer you to the right job but will help you choose the best people with whom to work. The word conscious is important. We all have a good, if vague, idea of where we shine and where we don't. But it's usually easier, especially given the stresses and pressures of our daily lives, to brush aside what we perceive as negatives, or not to take responsibility for our strengths by pretending modesty. Unfortunately, those same pressures and stresses of the working world do not leave much margin for error. Without an honest appraisal of ourselves, we don't make the best use of our abilities or of those around us. We invite others to find our blind spots and perhaps take advantage of them, potentially damaging situations for us all.

Make a list of your personality traits as they might pertain to work. What pleases or upsets you about each? What embarrasses you? What do you wish you could change? You can divide the qualities roughly into the following categories:

- Interpersonal skills. Are you a leader or a follower? A listener or a talker? Which kinds of people do you prefer to be around? Why? Because they challenge you, or because they tend to follow your advice?
- Analytical qualities. Do you consider yourself to be intuitive or logical? Do you shoot from the hip or think things through? Are you all heart or all mind? Do you like solving problems that have been handed to you, or do you prefer initiating your own projects, letting others figure out the nuts and bolts?
- Where are you on the organizational scale? Is organization important in your job? Will you need organizational backup? Do you like detail, paperwork?

What is your ideal working environment? Honest answers to this question can help show you what you are comfortable with in a professional setting and give you further clues to your own personality traits and how to use them at work. |

A good way to begin answering this question is to imagine your ideal working environment, or professional heaven as it were. It is the kind of environment in which you think you operate best, which sets your creative juices flowing and keeps you motivated. It's an environment that is either filled with people or lacks them, or is someplace in-between. It's the kind of environment that allows you to work at peak capacity.

- Do you see yourself working best in solitude? Or do you love interacting with people, being on the phone all day, answering questions, giving orders, enjoying the pressure and excitement of it all?

- Are you most comfortable with a laissez-faire type environment, where rules and regulations can be bent or even broken as long as the work gets done? Or do you prefer a little more rigidity, fearing that too much laissez-faire can bring about chaos?
- Do you like a working environment with much stability and quiet, knowing that everything is in its place, or do you prefer an atmosphere of creativity, where you can spend your time throwing out ideas and procedures, leaving it for others to do any cleaning up?
- Do you prefer a smaller, less formal office or a more corporate one?

Obviously, very few jobs are completely one thing or another. But as your responsibilities increase, as you hire employees and manage departments, you will be creating the environment in which you work. And although to a certain extent you will have to tailor your environment to that of the company, as a manager you will have the authority and the ability to create your own. The sooner you start thinking of these questions, and the more realistically you let the answers influence your choices, the better a fit you and your job will be.

What are your values? Values are your definition of who you are. And the combined values of all a firm's employees become a definition of what the firm is. While it is easy to think of values as something personal that should not intrude into the workaday world, the fact is they do, every day, all the time. A look at any debate surrounding a Supreme Court nominee proves it.

Just as you do an inventory of your personality traits and

office habits, you should also make a checklist of your values. Do you agree with Vince Lombardi that "Winning isn't everything. It's the only thing"? Do you believe that being fair and nice is much more important than achievement? Where are you on the lying/cheating scale? The aggressiveness scale? It's easy to say that you believe in always being fair and never lying, but the truth of the matter is that it's never black and white. How much quality are you willing to sacrifice for speed or quantity? Do you feel you are beginning to make too many compromises in these areas?

And you should be aware of the values of your company. Do they match yours? If they don't, how serious do you think the gaps are? Are they enough to make you want to change your job, or even the industry in which you work? How about the values of your co-workers? Do you feel comfortable with them? Although you can't expect everybody to think and act in the same way, a certain amount of agreement on principles may unite everyone and help create common goals that everyone can share.

What are your hidden prejudices? Although we all like to think we are models of enlightened citizenry, the truth of the matter is we all have our biases. When you look beyond the more obvious aspects of prejudice, you will be surprised at what you uncover. You as manager don't want these hidden prejudices to stand in your way and cause you to dismiss someone's skills and abilities because of factors that have nothing to do with work. These prejudices can be related to such factors as the following

- Age: Older workers are more conscientious than younger ones, although they don't perform as well; the older worker is less willing to change
- Sex: Women will get pregnant and leave; women are

more emotional and therefore less reliable than men; men are not as moody
- The disabled: Anyone with a physical disability can't perform up to peak capacity
- Nationality: Asians are good with technical knowledge but are not good leaders; immigrants from third-world countries don't have as good a work ethic as those of industrialized nations
- Speech: Anyone with a regional accent is not as intelligent as a person without one
- Looks: Beauty or ugliness are somehow related to work capability

Janet was going through a difficult period in her life: A successful copywriter for a top-notch magazine, she was breaking off a long-term relationship, helping her mother get through a serious illness, and at the same time trying to clear up some financial problems of her own. During this period, she found out that her trustworthy assistant was leaving. Janet did what she had always done in hiring someone: she chose a young woman with a most interesting background and keen intelligence, someone she knew wouldn't be satisifed with the job as it was but who would challenge her, creating a really dynamic team. After a few months' working with this person, however, Janet realized that the person was a little too challenging. Janet was still exhausted from dealing with all her serious personal problems, and while she'd always prided herself on doing a good job, during this period she could not give very much extra. Tension developed. Janet felt angry at her assistant's constant badgering and refusal to leave well enough alone; her assistant felt unappreciated and soon quit.

This story raises an interesting issue: Know what you want from your assistant. While we all agree that we should hire the "best" person available, the best is not a fixed entity.

Indeed, the same person can be great at one point in your professional career, and not so great at another. While most cases are not as extreme as Janet's, ask yourself the questions that follow whether you are hiring a new assistant or trying to work out your relationship with the person who works for you now. Apply what you learn from honestly answering these questions and come to an understanding with the person or persons who work for you. It will greatly reduce stress between you, as you will not expect things that this person is not prepared to give.

What do you expect your assistant to do? There are two parts to this question: The first has to do with how you think your assistant should *complement* your job. Is he or she primarily a secretary, a go-fer, or someone who will help you think, someone who will be doing projects independently of you? How you assistant's job complements yours, of course, depends on the nature of your job. Is it going through changes? Do you want to take it in a different direction perhaps, so that a shift will occur in what is required of each of you? Or as in Janet's case, do you want things to be steady for a while, your assistant efficiently doing what is required, no more no less?

Then, think of the *skills* that are most important to you. A good phone manner? Presentation skills? Being good with details? Fast typing or word processing ability? Good writing skills? Do you need a person with proven leadership ability to take over when you are gone? Someone to assist you on projects; someone who works well independently? While ideally you want an assistant who can do everything, chances are whoever you hire will be stronger in some areas, weaker in others.

And think of the hidden, little things that may be important to you. Do you need the person to be good at

screening phone calls or interruptions because making yourself too available to everyone is a particular weakness of
yours? Are you trying to make yourself computer literate?
Do you want an assistant whose skills can help you on that
score?

Certainly, all of a person's skills are not going to be
apparent when you interview them or when you first start
working together. But you can gauge their strengths and
watch what happens as you give them certain tasks. You can
encourage an assistant in areas that you think are important,
point out areas where you think there are problems. Or you
may find that what you thought was important is not so
important anymore because of other skills the person pos-
sesses. The trick is in being aware of what you expect at any
given moment so that you can communicate it in the best
possible manner.

What personal qualities do you value most in an employee?
While we are trained to think in terms of job descriptions and
skills as far as our assistants are concerned, we often forget
that something else comes into play: personal characteris-
tics. They are what determine how the person interacts with
you and other workers, and how they use their skills. Think
of the atmosphere your assistant will be working in and the
most common demands you will be placing on them. Then
make an appraisal of the qualities they would need most to do
the best job for you.

Qualities to consider are

- independence
- inquisitiveness
- a challenging spirit
- aggressiveness
- creativity

- stability
- perseverance
- a cheerful, optimistic disposition
- a quiet and obliging manner
- a different background to bring new insights

What is your relationship to your employee? This question can also be phrased, what do you think the employee expects from you? Are you to be

- a parent,
- a sibling,
- a friend,
- a nurturer,
- a teacher,
- or the terrible swift sword of justice?

The way you behave toward your employees will influence their behavior. Your employee takes her guidance from you—your tone, your manner of working, giving instructions, and relating to other employees and departments. In truth, you are a combination of all of the above factors, and consciously or not, you will choose which aspects of the relationship to emphasize, which to denigrate. By your choices, you will affect your assistant's responses to you, her job, and herself. If you're always telling her what to do and how to do it, don't be surprised that she doesn't make too many decisions on her own—even if she may be so inclined in the beginning. If you become chummy towards your employee, trading stories that have nothing to do with work, don't be surprised that when the time comes, exerting your authority might be difficult. If you are quick to point out inadequacies, don't expect those who work for you to be open with problems they may be having.

Some Notes on Hiring

You have been careful to determine the requirements of the job you want to fill, how it will complement yours, and what kinds of qualities may be most desirable in the person you are trying to hire. Now comes the hiring process itself. Your candidates will come to you via

- resumes that either you or the personnel department has on file
- word of mouth from friends or work contacts
- employment agencies, newspaper advertisements, etc.

No one source is necessarily a more reliable source than the others. A resume can look wonderful, but when you meet someone they can seem wrong for the job almost immediately. The good word from a work colleague helps, but doing well in a previous job or company is no guarantee of success in another. While many employment agencies have bad reputations, a good placement agent can do a wonderful job of matching applicants for jobs. All you can do is weigh your requirements against an applicant's concrete achievements (degrees, previous jobs, skills) and the chemistry that you feel when someone walks in for an interview.

Chemistry is that undefinable, all-important phenomenon that you should pay attention to carefully. During the interview, let your "gut" guide you. If the resume seems impressive, but some vague feeling tells you that something isn't right, listen to it; if the opposite happens—so-so resume but good chemistry—don't dismiss the person without giving a second look. Remember that certain skills can be taught, while basic personality doesn't change. And watch for pressure from bosses and colleagues to hire someone. If you feel you haven't found someone appropriate, don't settle. Have reasons handy why you can't find someone, but in the end, follow that gut.

As far as the interview itself is concerned, try to keep the atmosphere relaxed. It will help the person to open up and you to ask questions and evaluate the responses. Also,

- Know who you are interviewing. Study the resume, go over it in your mind right before the interview so you can ask specific questions.

- Give the person an overview of the job and what you expect from them. You can also use this opportunity to put the interviewee further at ease.

- Stay away from leading questions, such as "Are you organized?" which can only prompt an obvious "yes." Instead, ask open questions, such as "What do you feel are your strengths? Weaknesses?"

- Try to have a conversation. Pick things in the person's experience—a job, a school, a hobby—that you can identify with, and share experiences. The more someone talks, rather than merely answering questions, the more you can see what excites them, how they operate.

- Answer any of their questions about the job honestly. Don't misrepresent it to make it sound more interesting or responsible. At the same time, however, don't forget to point out the possibilities that the job can offer further down the road as a career stepping-stone, or as a way of getting a foot in the door.

- In the end, fitting a person to a job is always a guess, but you can make it an educated one by taking your own needs into careful consideration, having a realistic view of the job's demands, and understanding the kind of person required to cope with those demands.

2

...

Your Role as Manager: The Bigger Picture

You've given yourself a good once-over, and thought about your strengths, weaknesses, and your relationship to anyone you may be managing. Now it is time to think about some of the aspects of the manager's job. What makes a manager a manager? What distinguishes this person from other employees? What is this person's primary duty?

The primary duty is to get others to do things that you deem important. But how best to do this? A manager is one who is rising in the firm where he or she works, coming into contact with more and more people and learning more so that he can become responsible for its overall operations. But becoming responsible for more without giving up previous duties is not humanly possible.

Yet that is the problem many managers have. Even with evidence that it doesn't have to be this way, the image of the overwhelmed manager taking work home in a briefcase and staying at the office until all hours, has insinuated itself into the public consciousness, so much so that it makes many intelligent, capable people say that the last thing they want to do is take on the responsibilities of being a manager.

In order to be a good manager, you must accept your added responsibilities yet remain human at the same time. The five guidelines set forth here should help you as you hone your skills, delineate your duties, and learn how not to sell yourself short. They should convince you that thinking like a manager is the first step to being one.

A Manager Sees
The Bigger Picture

You as manager see how things work together, how people and issues act upon each other to create the unique challenges you face in your job. You may listen to one person's complaints and agree that they are legitimate. However, you also have to listen to opposing thoughts, which may be legitimate too. How do you choose a course of action? You look at the bigger picture.

And because you see the bigger picture you become responsible for it. Some of this happens automatically, as your new duties give you new knowledge that allows you to see things from different perspectives. But it also requires a conscious effort; you have to try not to get bogged down in old routines or stuck to old points of view. You take your old tasks and old routines and put them together with new tasks, paying attention to how they come together to form a whole. You have to remember that your company is now paying you to use your knowledge of the bigger picture to its fullest.

For someone who has been promoted, or someone who has particular expertise in a given area, paying attention to the bigger picture can be very difficult. For example, a crackerjack publicist is promoted to the head of a department. Everyone knows what a good job he did promoting the products of his firm and getting contacts, and he is proud of his accomplishments and the reputation he built up in the field. He also has confidence in the old job. Wanting to continue doing well, he creates a very open door in his department, allowing the younger publicists access to answer their questions and help resolve problems they may be having with their jobs.

All this is well and good. The danger is that his door will be too open, and as he concentrates on the old familiar tasks that reinforce his self-confidence, he will shy away from really tackling new problems that are surfacing. Perhaps his department has staffing problems. Or perhaps the way his predecessors have spent money doesn't work anymore. Or perhaps the whole nature of publicity is changing and he has to rethink some of the department's overall goals.

What he needs to do is make the bigger picture his first priority. Spend time thinking about what may be done. Have an ear to what is going on in the industry. It may mean the door has to stay closed more often, but he will be concentrating his energies on what his company is paying him for.

A Manager Has a Vision

It doesn't matter whether you are president of a big conglomerate or an average middle manager, you should have an idea of what you want to do with your job. Visions aren't only for saints. That is something we all tend to forget. Naturally, the higher your title, the broader your perspective, the bigger your vision is going to be. But wherever you are on the totem pole, you should have a long-range plan for your job, or your department, or your company. It allows you to prioritize, to make choices, to not get caught up in the daily minutiae that can blind you to what you really want to accomplish. It is a time map so you can do what you need to do without getting lost.

Suppose you are the vice president in charge of product development. One of your managers comes to you with an idea for a new product. It's hot, the public is craving it, you'll make a million bucks. Are you to pursue it? The immediate impulse seems to be yes, that's what you're here for, to pick up on trends and make the bottom line look good. But does this product fit in with your long-range plans? What if the money you allocate to it won't be available for something else? Is that okay with you? What do you want to produce? Will these products keep you in business?

Similar questions come up at all levels of management. Granted, a decision by a supervisor or middle manager may not mean much in the big scheme of things, but in aggregate these decisions mean a lot whether it's deciding how strict you will be regarding punctuality to what problems you will fight most to where you will concentrate your energies— having a vision will allow you to make the appropriate choices.

What follows is a list of questions you can ask yourself as you are thinking about your own vision for your job. As always, use them as guidelines. You may not be the head of a company, but you will have to make similar decisions as to how your job fits in with others in your firm, what you like or don't like about it, and where you may want it to lead.

- What is happening in the industry? In your company? Your job?
- Do you like the way things are going, or do you think there should be a change?

- If you think change is necessary, what can you do in your job to influence this?
- Is the focus of your job too scattered? Should you concentrate more on one area?
- Should your job have a broader focus or more authority? Why?
- How will the people you manage fit in with these changes?
- What changes do you think should be made first?

A Manager Makes
Time to Contemplate

The higher someone is on the managerial totem pole, the more important it is that he or she make time for contemplating. Yet, the higher one is on the totem pole, the harder it is to find the time for it.

Managing means dealing with different personalities. It also means seeing to the "regular" work that needs to be done. These two factors play upon one another and create endless distractions and problems to be solved—if the manager will allow it. The manager can spend his entire day, and more, solving and re-solving matters and still feel that very little has been accomplished.

To counteract these forces, it is very important to set aside a certain portion of the day for thinking. This "quiet time" is a way of distancing yourself a bit from all those immediate distractions. It will allow you to recharge your batteries, see things in a different perspective, and bring your familiarity with the bigger picture and your vision into the forefront of your activities. It is certainly not fluff time, but time for real pondering, problem solving, and taking a look at that long-range plan for your job, which nobody else can do for you. And it is a demonstrated fact that as you let your mind concentrate on something else, those immediate problems will come into better focus, so when you do go back to solving them you will be much more effective at doing so.

For most people, this thinking time is best done sometime in the morning, when the distractions are minimal and your energies are at their peak. Doing it early in the day has another advantage: Experience has shown the time experts that one should complete the most important tasks first, otherwise, it's just too easy to have the day run away from you, as the distractions mount and the pressure increases. It's not a weakness on your part, it's human nature. But studying human nature has also shown us how much people vary. If your energies peak at noon or sometime after noon, set aside the time then. The important thing is that you designate a certain block of time as devoted to contemplation and nothing else. It is a way of acknowledging the importance of this activity, giving it the same priority as time set aside for marketing sessions and organizational meetings.

Acknowledging the importance of contemplation is also the reason you do it during your working day. If you do it at home, or on the train, or here and there when the spirit moves you, you are telling yourself and others that it's not quite as important on your agenda as other demands.

Many managers fear that contemplation means cutting themselves off from their co-workers. Shutting the office door goes against the grain of our open-door policy of office life (which to us means people working together and having a manager as teacher and support system). It seems to be a sign of disrespect. But think of it this way: It is a sign of disrespect to the position not to devote some time to thought. If you have a trustworthy assistant who's good at screening, the door doesn't have to be closed. If you don't and a closed door is your only way to privacy, coming to an understanding with everyone ahead of time is a way to solve the problem. As always, it is a matter of balance. If your door is always shut, that will indeed be disrespectful to your co-workers. If it is shut for an hour or so each day, with the recognition that you need this time to plan and think, it will only be a healthy sign of respect for yourself.

A Manager Sets
Goals and Priorities

Goal setting and prioritization are ways of planning for the future and using your knowledge of the bigger picture and your vision to get you where you think you should be. Goal setting takes that knowledge and focuses it on specific accomplishments that you expect of yourself and your job over a given period of time.

When you sit down to think through your goals, focus on your long-term purpose first. You should think of it as one overall goal you want to achieve. Those who report to you should have more distinct responsibilities. There should be less paperwork in your job. Your company should grow by X percent. This may be weeks, months, or years away. Nevertheless, it is important to start with this because it will influence the other, shorter term goals that derive from this one.

The shorter term goals will be more numerous and will also be apt to shift more. Even if your overall purpose has remained the same, your shorter term goals will change as you adapt to circumstances around you. Adaptability is vital. Life—and certainly the working world—isn't static and you must be prepared to change your goals if you feel this is warranted. To use Ralph Waldo Emerson's words in his famous essay on self-reliance, "A foolish consistency is the hobgoblin of little minds." The balance between adaptability and perseverance is a fine one, and the only way to keep it is by a continual testing of the waters.

Go through a mental checklist of the following questions to help yourself as you refine and prioritize your goals:

- What needs to be done? Start with what you think is the most important—this will be your overall goal. Then prioritize downward.
- Why should you do it? Be clear on this, as it is the reason for your setting the goal in the first place. You may discover you are setting the wrong goal because your reasons for setting it are not really justified.
- Who should do it? Does it only involve you, or others who work with you or report to you? This means being clear on who does what and being prepared to make changes as necessary.
- How long it will take to be done? Though nothing in life seems to be more unpredictable than how long something takes to do, you should try to give your best approximation.
- When should it be done? Compare it to what else you're doing or planning to do, remembering to allot enough time and resources for both.
- How should it be done? You won't know all the answers to this one, yet you will have some ideas based on all the other factors involved. This question may come up frequently during times of change, and that is why continual reappraisal of it all on a scheduled basis is so necessary.

A Manager Makes Decisions

A telling exchange between two soldiers occurs during a ferocious battle in *Apocalypse Now,* Francis Ford Coppola's vision of the hell that was Vietnam. The hero, a captain played by Martin Sheen, is desperately trying to acclimate himself to the situation. Coming upon a soldier cowering in a foxhole, he asks him who's in charge. "I thought you were," replies the soldier, cowering even more.

A similar dilemma seems to face many managers in the workplace. As they run around trying to fix problems, to respond to crises, and to keep juggling all the things that are demanded of them, they often forget that they are in charge. It is up to them to make decisions and take responsibility for them.

Decision making is frightening at first, because like the captain in *Apocalypse Now,* one is acutely aware of how little one knows about what is going on. The events swirling around may seem terrifying and confusing, but a decision has to be made. The first step is to overcome that fear and make the best decision one can. To their great relief, most new managers realize that no one has questioned their decision. It has not caused any horrible repercussions. They make more, and the more decisions they are able to make, the more they can put them in perspective. Slowly, over time, they let their experience guide them and are able to make bigger decisions with greater consequences.

Thinking of yourself as a decision maker is also a reminder that a manager acts—as opposed to reacting to events. It means taking an active role in the goings-on and shows that you trust yourself enough to come up with questions and solutions to propel your company further, get things done, and influence your fellow employees. It doesn't mean that you don't listen to anyone else; on the contrary, it means you are more able to work with others, as you are not afraid to take in more bits of information and make decisions based on them.

And it helps you deal with crises. If someone runs into your office and cries that something terrible has just happened, what may seem catastrophic to this person may not seem so horrible when seen from another perspective. Not jumping on the bandwagon immediately is a way to calm someone down, even as you fully acknowledge their fear and the very real problems they may be having.

In the end, it seems to be this calming influence that is most appreciated by those you manage. You may be at wit's end trying to deal with ten things at once, but those you manage are dealing with a multitude of problems also. The least you can do is present a stabilizing influence, using your prior experience and knowledge that it all somehow works out. Pass this knowledge on. It will help all of you get through the day.

Part II

. . . . .

The Tools of
Managing

3

...

Communication: Never Assume Anything

"Never assume anything," should be every manager's philosophy. It expresses the feeling that in dealing with people, you don't take anything for granted. It means realizing that those you manage are not a part of you. They are separate human beings who may not understand or even care what you are trying to accomplish. The first step in bridging this gap and getting things done is communication.

Communication is your primary management tool; it is how you put across who you are, what you do, and what you wish to have done. And it is how you appreciate and learn to pay attention to those you work with. A breakdown in work flow is often simply a problem in communication. Once the various parties really talk to each other, the problems get cleared up and the work flows with a minimum of fuss.

Listening

Communication begins with listening effectively to those you work with. Effective listening has two components: First, it means finding out what it is that these people are trying to communicate to you. Second, it is a way of showing them that you care about them and their work.

Think of the last time someone rushed into your office and delivered a request or spilled out a problem. Did you feel forced to listen, or were you genuinely interested? Were you happy with the way you dealt with the situation or do you think you got bogged down in trivialities? Your answer will probably be much more positive if you were an active participant rather than a passive observer. It's an important distinction to keep in mind: Good listening is active, not passive. It means you pay attention. It means you have the strength to stay with the person, absorbing what they have to say and giving yourself time to think through what it means. Then you respond accordingly.

To be an attentive listener first learn to gauge what you are listening to. Is the problem real, or is the person trying to kill time? Sometimes co-workers only need to get something off their chest, or to tell an anecdote to break some tension that may exist between the two of you (either due to a past problem or a current difficulty). If it's the former, decide whether you have time to listen. At the same time, remember that solving a concrete work problem is not the only reason you pay attention; acknowledging the other person with a few minutes of your time can be an important motivational tool.

To help yourself listen, learn to ask questions before you give answers. Why does someone need something? Does it have to be done now? Who's involved in the particular situation? Can it be looked at in another way? Your questions are a good way of clarifying problems and leading the person to their own solutions. More important, they are a good way of finding out what's really on someone's mind.

Within the first few minutes, you will know whether or not you want to listen further. If you don't, it's important to communicate this as soon as you've decided. It can be done in a nice but firm way, honestly saying that something else takes precedence. Setting a time in the future to deal with the particular issue at hand is certainly acceptable to most people. Cutting short a social conversation with a chronic talker, however, is easier said than done. In your own office, you can use the hint of getting up at your desk to signal that listening time is over. If you need a stronger hint pick up the phone, or even go to your door, excusing yourself politely but also signaling that you have to go somewhere.

Once you've made the decision to listen, there are some small pointers you can use to make sure you are meeting your goals of finding out information and acknowledging the speaker:

- Look at the person. It doesn't mean staring at them fixedly but honest eye-to-eye contact. This is not the time to look around the room or stare into space or look down at your desk for long periods. Remember, at this point you are not solving something, you are trying to hear what someone has to say.
- You can't listen and chew gum at the same time. Don't do two things at once. If you're feeling pressured, it's sometimes tempting to think about that memo you have to write to your boss as you're listening to why your assistant can't get the accounts receivable department to return his phone calls. Don't do it. You won't do either task well, and your assistant deserves your full attention.

- Keep focused. If you're tired, keeping your mind from wandering is even more difficult. Watch out for those glassy eyes, that bored look, the slumped posture. They will be noticed immediately and will send out signals that you don't want to hear what the speaker has to say.
- Know when to interrupt. Don't jump in unless you feel the person isn't making any sense or is repeating himself. Letting someone finish gives both of you an opportunity to relax and keep the exchange flowing.
- Don't stop listening when someone "higher up" pops by or calls. This is an important one because it is so insidious. We often have a tendency to automatically ignore the employee for a boss—or a peer if the speaker is an assistant or a secretary—because we quickly assume that the other person has something more important to say. You will obviously have to judge by the situation and the persons involved but the point is, don't make it automatic. Nothing is more disheartening to someone than to be subjected to repeated interruptions.
- As a final point, it is just good to remember what a soothing effect listening provides—for all of us. It breaks the psychic walls people have built up between each other and reminds them that they are not alone in dealing with the day-to-day problems all of us face. Knowing that someone will listen if the problem becomes too great fulfills a very real need.

Saying No Effectively

Both on a small and big scale, one of the most difficult things a manager has to cope with is saying no. Whether it's saying no to a bigger raise, or no to a new office, or no to leaving early, it's never pleasant. But it doesn't have to be traumatic either. Being firm but gentle (i.e. honest but caring) works best. Here are some guidelines for saying no.

- Show that you are sympathetic to the request. There will probably be some merit in what someone is asking of you. Acknowledge this.
- Use your knowledge of the bigger picture. Usually you will have to say no because of other factors that the person is not aware of. Point them out.
- Be honest. Don't make up excuses. They snowball, and they are more transparent then you realize.
- Know your authority. If your decision is overturned, it can undermine your position. If it happens often, you lose all credibility. If you know that your word may not be final, say no, while informing the person that they can go to someone higher if they disagree strongly. It leaves you with an out.
- Be careful that you are not just saying no to prove your power. Saying no should not be a game of power or anything else; if you can't think of an adequate reason, maybe you should say yes.

Losing Your Temper

An occasional display of temper is sometimes a very important tool of communication. *Display* is the key word here. Always lose your temper with your emotions in control! Does it sound like a contradiction? It isn't. All it means is that you are angry and feel that your anger is justified because you sense a particular apathy in the people you are managing—you've had to repeat yourself because no one is paying attention, discipline has slacked off, morale is low, no one seems to care—at that point you let out your anger. You do so because you want to prove that you care! But you have have to

- use it very sparingly
- be honestly angry
- never be abusive or insulting
- make it brief

And as with any criticism, you are always specific in what you single out, and you focus on the work, not the person.

Nonverbal Impressions

Every day you give impressions of yourself to your co-workers, impressions that you communicate nonverbally. They are important because they are what stick in someone's mind; once formed they are hard to change, whether right or wrong. Someone's impression of you defines what they think of you, which in turn affects how they respond to you. The impression you give of yourself will set the tone of your relationships with your co-workers and will affect the give and take of the work itself.

Go through the following list and make yourself aware of how the impressions you generate determine your effectiveness as a manager:

- Self-esteem. It comes across in how you carry yourself, how you dress, what you say, what you really think of yourself, and very important, how you respond to not knowing an answer. Having the self-confidence to admit not knowing something and then being able to find out if necessary, is much more a sign of self-assurance than a lack of capability.

- Strength of purpose. You should be thought of as sticking to your guns and knowing what you want. Again, it doesn't mean not changing your mind if new evidence warrants it. It means not giving in to threats or intimidation or favoritism.
- Stability. A manager should come across as someone fairly stable, not saying and doing one thing one day in a given situation and then doing something totally different the next. Unpredictability makes those who work for you mistrustful and those who work above you doubt your abilities.
- Hypocrisy. The golden rule applied to managers: If you're in a position of authority, doing unto yourself not like you do unto others is very tempting—the perks are greater, the controls fewer, the opportunities more apparent. Fortunately (or unfortunately—depending on your point of view!) insincerity makes itself known sooner or later. If that label is applied to you, your efforts at getting things done and motivating others are for naught. Their respect for you is gone.
- Organization. Companies are called organizations for a reason. With so many people working together, certain regulations and procedures have to be followed so that everybody can communicate as efficiently as possible. Many disorganized managers solve the problem by making sure their assistants and secretaries do the organizing for them. That is legitimate—up to a point. Your own disorganization puts a great strain on your support staff, and it is very irritating to your co-workers (not to mention your bosses) when you (or your assistant) can't locate a file or forget to return phone calls. Thinking your

assistant will do it all, while you pride yourself on other aspects of your job, is a dangerous trap that often turns into bigger problems.

- Optimism. You don't have to be Pollyanna, but nothing will undermine your credibility more than always being pessimistic. Even if times are difficult, constantly walking around disparaging everything, saying things won't work out, acting as though the end of the world is near will not win you any points with your colleagues and will totally demoralize your staff. If you find yourself complaining all the time, sit down and think through why. If there are things that can be changed, do so; otherwise, perhaps it is time to look for another job.

- Bluster. There are those managers who love to intimidate the people who work for them and yet who cater to every whim of their own boss. Although it may take a while, staff usually catch on to this and resent it tremendously. They rightfully see the intimidation as the only way a manager can soothe his bruised ego because he is afraid to stand up to his own boss. It is one thing to motivate your staff to please the wishes of a tough boss, but do not play games with them, act tough for its own sake, or think that being difficult or unreasonable will make them respect you. On the contrary, they will see through it and respect you less than if you had openly acknowledged the difficulty of a particular situation and asked everybody for their help in pitching in.

Apart from the nonverbal impressions you give, you also communicate with your fellow employees directly, whether verbally or in written form. You should think of such communication as revealing your feelings as honestly as possible without trampling on the rights of others. It is not always easy, but both are possible. No matter what situation you are in, there are general rules for all to follow in this regard.

Always be clear when communicating. It seems so easy to forget that if you're not clear about what you want to say no one else will be either. Sort it through beforehand. Also, be concise. Being a manager doesn't mean you are a robot that gives dry responses or one-line commands, but going on and on at length shows disrespect for someone else's time and your own position.

Flying off the handle isn't a very good idea either. Your co-workers want to feel that you think before you talk. Flip remarks, sarcastic comments, and flashes of anger have their place, but not at the expense of thoughtful comment. This is where you can really get in trouble with others' sensibilities.

Remember also that in talking with an assistant or an employee, how much your authority magnifies even the smallest thing you say. Your voice, your demeanor, everything carries extra weight because of your position. If you criticize work that your assistant has done, keep your perspective. Understand how much power you have in such a situation. Although it isn't always necessarily so, by virtue of your position you are assumed to have more knowledge and experience. And because you can fire or recommend this person for other positions, he wants to please you. Tread carefully.

Giving Feedback

Praising or criticizing an employee is called "giving feedback." Giving about four to five times more praise than criticism is a good rule of thumb to follow. If this ratio seems askew, perhaps you are being unreasonable or your employee really is performing below par. In either case, some changes will have to be made.

In terms of giving feedback, here are some tips to remember:

- Be specific. It will be important for your assistant to know exactly what he did right or wrong. Extra words will just be confusing.
- Don't wait to give either praise or criticism—do it right away. Pointing out something when it happens is a much better way to teach then saving it up. Also, constant praise is reassuring; too much criticism at once is demoralizing. It makes it that much harder for someone to learn from mistakes, which is the purpose of criticism.
- Always think of criticism as constructive. Encouragement and positive approval are always more effective teaching tools than negative criticism.
- Don't praise or criticize the person, only the work itself. Concentrate on the job. You have no right to judge someone's qualities, as in "You're not very logical." Instead, in that particular situation you may say, "You didn't put down the points in a logical order because of such and such."
- If you're criticizing something, make sure it's possible to change it. If your assistant is in charge of collecting data from two different departments, don't criticize her tardiness if one of her sources is late. Acknowledge her lateness (you may question her or point it out), then check to see why the other department is not cooperating.

Think of it this way: In praising someone you are telling them to do more of the same thing. In criticizing, you want someone to stop doing something or to do it differently. In both cases you are encouraging them to grow.

The Performance Review

As one of your tasks in managing, you will be asked to give official performance reviews. Depending on your firm and the level of those you manage, the reviews will come once or twice a year. After talking to your subordinates, you will be asked to put something in writing. Here are some guidelines to follow for all such meetings:

- Don't solve specific work problems. You should look at a performance review as a balanced overview of the recent past. Talk over basic strengths and weaknesses with the person you are reviewing. Specific work problems can be brought up as they relate to the overall performance, but they should be worked out at another time.
- Don't make it a surprise. What you say should not be totally unexpected by your subordinate. If you've been giving the person ongoing feedback, they will have a pretty good idea of what to expect. This is the time for fine tuning and summing up.
- Set long-term goals. Use the opportunity to come up with long-term goals for your subordinate's job. Should she be doing more of one thing and less of another? Is he ready to take the job in a new direction?
- Always ask the employee for feedback. The employee should feel part of the process, and relaxed enough to let out feelings on how you perform toward them, how they think they are doing, and the goals

they want for their job. Getting some of this information may take some gentle prodding from you. If you sense that they can't talk about something this very minute, don't force them. Keep yourself open for when it does come up.

- At the end of the review, you both know where you stand. If all has gone well, you should each feel that you have a good understanding of the other and of your expectations for what each of you does or doesn't do.
- The employee should know what is going into the personnel files. They should be given a copy of anything you send to personnel or put on their record. It is a courtesy, allowing them to respond yet again, and it protects both of you in case of any problems later on.

Taking Criticism

It may not be pleasant, but it will happen: you will be on the receiving end of complaints or criticism. And it may not come from your colleagues or your boss—remember, your assistant or employee has a right to complain also. You owe them the courtesy of listening, as long as the complaining is work-related and not personal. If it becomes personal, insulting, or abusive in any way, you should terminate the conversation, saying you will be glad to listen when the person calms down. (Another all-purpose response if someone seems angry or out of control: tell them you don't think it is a good time to discuss the particular matter and leave it at that, letting them take the responsibility of coming back to you when they have settled down.)

In listening to someone's complaints, observe the following guidelines.

- Don't be defensive. Accept what they have to say without making excuses.
- Wait till they are finished to give your side of the story. In the first place, this allows you time to think. Also, it shows that you take their point of view seriously.
- If there is some truth to what they have to say, acknowledge it. This is especially true for someone who reports to you, so they know they are free to complain if they feel it is warranted.
- Watch out for subtle threats or intimidation. If you see them, point them out, which is a way of saying that you will not give in to them.
- Apologize if you feel it is appropriate.
- Try to come to some common resolution. Even if a problem hasn't been solved, you can agree on the points you will work on, and perhaps check back with each other at some future date.

Running a Meeting

The thing to remember about meetings is that their primary purpose is to facilitate communication. They exist to give employees a way of coming together and sharing information as efficiently as possible. Many managers spend fifty percent or more of their time in meetings, yet they often feel they have accomplished very little. You want to prevent this if you are running a meeting. To do so, think of running a meeting as having three stages:

- You have to adequately prepare for it.
- You have to take the responsibility for actually running, or directing, the meeting.
- You have to follow up carefully.

Prepare for a meeting before calling it, keeping in mind the following:

- Know what you want the meeting to accomplish. Make an agenda by listing the main points you want to bring up. Go over them before the meeting so they are clear in your mind.
- Know who should be there and why. If you have to, do some preparatory investigating to find out who does what, so that all topics that need to be discussed will be done so adequately.
- Keep it simple. Although you want all bases covered, be careful not to make the meeting too large. Chances are, the more people who participate, the less will get done. Pare down the topics if you find too many names on your list, and plan for a second meeting.
- Assign someone to take notes. You may wish to do so yourself if the meeting is fairly informal and small (no more than three or four colleagues). If the meeting is any larger or more formal, you will need someone else to do it, as you will be concentrating your energies on the work at hand.
- Check out any equipment you may be using beforehand! Malfunctioning slide projectors, VCRs, and tape recorders can spoil many a good effort.

In terms of time, you should plan for nothing longer than an hour to an hour and a half. If the meeting has to run longer, institute breaks. Since you are running the meeting, use your own office space or a neutral meeting room—with you at the head of the table. Either way, it's an acknowledgment that you're in charge. And be very hesitant about canceling a meeting once you've set it, whether you are meeting with one person or many. Switching times or letting last-minute pressures delay or cancel meetings simply says that you find something else more worthy of your attention than somebody else's valuable time. If you have to cancel make sure that it is a real emergency.

At the meeting itself, you speak first. Make any introductions that may be needed; this will be important if anyone from outside the company is attending. After stating the purpose of the meeting clearly and concisely, start going down your list and bring up issues and questions as you have prioritized them.

Besides discussing the issues at hand, you always have to be aware that you are *running* the meeting. You will be setting the tone for what transpires and directing the discussion. It also means you have a responsibility to

- keep things on track by following your agenda
- be aware of all the participants by letting everyone have their say
- stop a discussion if it's going on too long
- stop an argument if it becomes too spirited or personal
- draw out reticent participants by asking their opinion on specific matters
- don't let any one person monopolize the conversation
- watch the clock

At the conclusion, it is always a smart idea to summarize the meeting. Go over what has been discussed and decided, and get everybody's agreement. It is sometimes hard to do this for the simple reason that people are tired and want to leave. However, it is very important because it not only serves the purpose of quickly reiterating what has been accomplished, but it also acts as a safety net, catching anything that was left unclear or unresolved. As the primary purpose of the meeting should be communication, you want everybody to leave with a clear understanding of what went on and what still needs to be done.

After you return from the meeting you should make sure that formal minutes are prepared. This should be done as soon after the meeting as possible, when the information is fresh and most accessible.

Memos

What would we do without memos? We write them to publicize information, give orders, point out problems, vent frustration, announce comings and goings, and perhaps most important, to cover our precious behinds. But do we read them?

That is the number one point you should keep in mind whenever you are writing a memo: it is meant to be read—usually by someone who is rushed and only interested in very specific bits of information. With that in mind, here are some points to consider.

- Be clear on what information you are trying to convey, which partly depends on who is getting the memo. What particular facts are important to them? How many? Be careful of including too much background information, overexplaining a certain problem, or justifying why you are writing the memo.
- Less is more. This saying is particularly true of memos. The general rule of thumb is no more than a page in length, often just a paragraph or two. If you find yourself writing more, take a second look. You may need to do some editing; or what you are

actually writing is a report or a study, which is something else entirely.

- Use underlining, indentation, and bullets for quick visual access to your most important points. The easier they are to read, the more you will find that people actually respond.
- Organization, organization, organization. Even a short memo needs thought and a logical sequence. A memo is a finished product; so unless you are one of those rare human beings who can do both simultaneously, think it through before you write it.
- Forget about humor. Don't try to be flip or funny. While humor enhances things when you are dealing with people face to face, as odd as it may seem, it has the opposite effect in memos. It makes it seem as though you are not taking the memo reader or the situation seriously enough.
- Use one memo per problem, not ten memos per person. If ten people need to know about a particular problem, think through the basics of what they need to know and put that information in one memo. Try to avoid writing separate memos as much as possible. This not only cuts down on your work but also everyone will have one standard piece of paper to refer to later on.
- Know who is supposed to get the memo and make sure it gets there! More problems in corporate America seem to be caused by people claiming never to have received a memo than anything else. Cover yourself by finding out who is supposed to get memos on various topics and keep the list handy.

Gossip

If you want information to be passed on as quickly as possible, just tell a trusted friend at work that a piece of news is confidential and not to be shared with anyone else. It's quicker than a fax.

4

...

Delegating:
The Art of Letting Go

Delegating is letting go. It means recognizing that you are being paid to do the job of a manager and that assistants and other employees are being paid to support you in your work. It means recognizing that everyone has responsibilities. It is up to you to decide where those responsibilities fall, not only between you and your assistants, but also within the overall scheme of the firm. You have to decide how much work to accept and when, and how to direct it. You have draw the lines of authority and make sure they are being followed. As manager, both the work and the work flow are your responsibility.

This, of course, doesn't mean that you do all the work yourself. Successful delegating begins with the assumption that you cannot do it all. As simple as it may sound, it is also the most difficult thing for many managers to accept. Yet, letting go of the old job and learning to accept the new one is the crux of growing as a manager.

Letting go includes trust. One must learn how to let others do the old job while you concentrate on new tasks and new management skills. It is easy to sabotage that trust by the old no-one-can-do-it-as-well-as-I-can routine—and it is probably true. Because of your experience and particular talents, maybe no one can do it as well, and maybe no one will for a long time. That must be accepted. In the greater scheme of things, it is more important that you do your new job and that whoever has taken over your old one does theirs.

In letting go, you also acknowledge how much fear you may have about the new job. Understand that it's a natural response. You're at your new desk or in your new office and suddenly the whole world seems to be coming to you with questions and problems. Your first tendency is to want your old job back or do things the tried-and-true way; after all, you've learned that it works. Change is frightening, whether you're taking your first baby steps or sitting in on your first board meeting.

You also want your assistants to grow. Remember, part of your job as manager is being responsible for those who work under you. What you want, they want. What you fear, they fear. Just as you do at a different level, they need to become more confident and try new things. They need to feel that trust.

Acknowledging Mistakes

Inevitably, trying new things in new ways will sometimes result in mistakes. We all make mistakes and we all feel bad about them. Yet part of the trust involved in delegating is allowing for that possibility, both for yourself and for those who report to you. Looking at mistakes in such a way is productive, rather than inhibiting. It is an acknowledgment that everyone makes mistakes and an encouragement not to be afraid to take on more responsibility. As manager, it is up to you create such an atmosphere by

- making it known that honest mistakes are not only tolerated but welcome
- admitting when you have made a mistake
- being positive when critiquing an honest mistake

If you have asked an assistant to be more creative in her job and she does something new that does not work, first praise her efforts at being creative. If there was a good aspect to what she tried to do, by all means point it out. Then point out why in this particular instance her overall efforts were misguided. Finish your exchange by telling her again to keep trying different angles. If you merely correct the problem or show irritation, she will not think your dictum to be more creative was meant sincerely, and she will feel more inhibited in the future.

By all means, however, point out careless mistakes and laziness. And don't pretend indifference. If you honestly feel so, tell your employee when she makes you upset or frustrated, that you want a better performance from her, that you hired her with certain expectations that you do not think are being met.

Assigning Work

Successful delegation involves assigning work, giving directions as to how the work should be done, and making sure that the work is satisfactorily executed.

Before you assign work, however, you have to determine whether the work should be given away in the first place. Some people feel that managers should not do anything routine, and that anything repetitive (i.e. boring/uncreative) should be done by subordinates. Others use the criterion on of menial labor. The problem is that definitions of routine and menial vary, and it is impossible for anyone to escape some routine at work. Whether or not you occasionally type your own letters is not the issue. The issue is judging what needs to be done and getting it done in the most effective way.

You may be assigning work to one person or five departments. Whichever it is, many of the same principles apply. Run through the following checklist of what you should keep in mind when you are assigning work:

- Relative importance. Ask yourself how a particular task or project fits within the larger scheme of things. Is it an extreme rush or just a regular rush? What are the consequences if it doesn't get done? How will its success or failure reflect on you?
- Timing. Keep a mental note of what other projects you have given to your assistant. If she has been with you a while and feels secure in her job, she will feel freer to tell you if she's doing something else that is taking up her time. A less confident person may find it harder to do so.
- Its difficulty. Even though you may not (and probably shouldn't) know the details of how the work gets done, you should have some idea of its complexity. If you don't, ask.
- Its duration. You should also have some idea of how long it should take. Making yourself generally aware of what's involved in completing a task falls right on that fine boundary line between your responsibilities

and those of the people you manage. Basic knowledge of what's involved shows that you care about their efforts.

- Why is it being done? Always ask yourself this question. If you do, you may be amazed by how often you are just passing on a request by a boss or colleague that really shouldn't be done at all. It's a function of being nice and pleasing people, and it can cost you and your assistant many hours better spent on other things.

Also, consider the "responsibility quotient" of the person to whom you are giving the work. Are they good at taking on projects like this? Will they consider this a chore or a challenge? How they react to it will have a bearing on how they carry it out, and how closely you will have to work with them.

You may find some people eager to give back any responsibility you hand over to them. They may interrupt you with questions more often than you feel is warranted. They may not make any decisions without checking with you first. Or their progress may make you realize that they are clearly uncomfortable with the work. You will have to determine whether they fear responsibility in general or the particular task you have given them. If it's the task, it may be that you were not clear enough in your instructions or handed over a little bit too much at once. If you don't think you have, if they seem to react the same way to any responsibility you give them, you will then have to determine whether you will live with the situation or try to get them to change.

Can you teach responsibility? Yes. Not taking responsibility usually masks fear. By using patience, giving encouragement, setting an example, and providing a supportive atmosphere, you can help someone gain confidence in their abilities. However, you have to remember that this takes time. The work you and your people are responsible for comes with pressures and deadlines. If someone is not ready, you cannot force responsibility on them. In a situation like that, determine how worthwhile the person's work is to you overall by weighing their other strengths versus the requirements of the job. If you feel you've tried and the person is not ready to take on the necessary responsibility, you are justified in seriously considering a replacement.

When you are assigning work to a number of people, all of the above concerns apply. However, because there is more than one person involved, you have a few other considerations:

- Ask yourself who is best suited for the job. In many cases this will be obvious. In others, you may have a choice. Think of both skills and experience, and weigh each accordingly.
- Personality is important also. Keep in mind the different quirks of your employees. Does he like a lot of running around? Is she introverted or extroverted? The job may involve working with other people. Is the person you've chosen a good match for them?
- Will it matter to your subordinates who gets the job? Is there competition among them? Is one doing more work than others? Be open to these possibilities, as they may save you listening to unnecessary complaining and reassigning the work later on.

Presenting Work

After you have decided upon the work you will be assigning, you have to present it to your subordinate, giving any instructions that may be necessary. At this point, also think back to the last time similar work was done. If you want something done more, or less, thoroughly, now is the time to say so. If you think your assistant did something particularly exemplary or neglectful the last time, you should remind them of it now, not when they hand you their work at the finish.

In presenting the work to your subordinate, follow these guidelines.

- Be prepared. If it's complex, run over the major aspects of the job in your own mind first to make sure you are clear on what you will be asking.
- In giving instructions, don't overdo it. You don't want to tell someone how to do something so that they have no room to make decisions on their own. Give the basics, first presenting the overall purpose of what is being done and then giving a rundown of the steps involved. If you need certain things done in a particular way, point this out, but don't go overboard. Too many instructions at once will seem overwhelming, and you want to give those you manage time to think and solve problems.
- Ask, don't demand. Asking is more polite because it shows respect. It's an acknowledgment that if your assistant really feels the need to, he can say no. It also helps him grow by having to think it through, no matter how momentarily, and then give you an answer.

You do, of course, have the option of not only demanding but commanding. You may do so if you are angry about previously sloppy work or if you are in a particularly stressful situation. However, remember the consequences. It may make your assistant work more quickly, though probably not more efficiently. If you're angry, your assistant will in turn be angry or frightened. If you are feeling pressured, remember the following: Don't snap and never yell. You will just make it worse. Take a minute to work out your own stress so that you don't pass it on.

There are a couple of other points to consider:

- Make sure that you're understood. If the task is important enough, you can ask your assistant to repeat what you've just told her. To avoid being patronizing, admit that you are having her do this because getting the work done correctly is important to you. And give the reasons.
- Be careful of being "yes-ed" to death. Yes, I can do this. Yes, it's no problem. Yes, I can do everything. It sounds good, but it means trouble. Even if you do give them the option, many people are afraid of saying no. Look beyond the yes responses to see if the person really means it. Ask what else they're doing. Find out how much they know about this particular task. And be aware of nonverbal cues like tentative responses or silence. These can tell you a lot.

Follow Up

In making sure that work is being done, your skills at letting go are really tested. The trick, of course, is in giving your assistant enough freedom to do the work, which means allowing for mistakes. But you can't afford total failure, either. Where do you draw the line?

Following up on work is never easy, and it's a problem

most managers wrestle with. Some let go of the work totally, then take it out on the assistant if a problem develops. On the opposite end are the control freaks who keep such tight tabs on the work that the assistant never feels trusted. Weigh the complexity and importance of the work against your assistant's experience and competence, and also keep in the mind the following:

- Understand how important it is for someone to feel that the project is their own. It means having pride in a job well done. If an assistant really feels in charge, they will invest more of themselves in it. Keep reminding yourself of this as you worry about how the job is going.
- Set up control points. They serve as a checkup on what's been done and give a green light to go further. They can be based on the following:

  - Time. You agree to discuss the work at certain prescheduled times
  - Different stages. You base your checking on different stages of the work being finished
  - Particular problems. You ask you assistant to see you if problems of a particular nature come up

- The important thing is to agree on the control points ahead of time. Scheduling in advance is important for two reasons: it assures that the checkup will take place, and it lessens stress. And discussing work on a particular schedule de-personalizes it. Your assistant knows he is coming to see you because it has been agreed beforehand, not necessarily because he isn't doing well. It also keeps interruptions to a minimum, which take both of you away from other work.

- Don't keep interrupting. Random checking up by you takes away from an assistant's feeling of being in charge. If you are worried, one reminder is fine. More should not be necessary.
- Don't take it back if it's going badly. Short of firing someone outright, it is the most demoralizing thing you can do. And you don't need the extra work. Redo something yourself only as a last resort. Try to help out first by working a little more closely with your assistant, asking more pointed questions, specifying problem areas in more detail.
- Have patience. If you've done something a hundred times you may have forgotten how difficult it was initially. As an exercise, take a task that you can do without thinking and recall the first time. Now put yourself in your assistant's shoes.
- Show encouragement—it's easy to forget and much appreciated. Saying, for example, "I can tell by the questions you're asking that you are going to do just fine," both encourages further questions and gives an assistant confidence.

A final word about setting deadlines, checking on delivery dates, and determining control points: Always set an exact date. If you are creating a deadline, never make it vague. If someone owes you work and you want to find out when it's coming, never accept "soon" as an answer. You may give them the choice of setting the time—in fact, that is preferable—but no matter who sets it, it should be specific. Pin them down. It will give them something to shoot for and it gives you a hook, a time for making further plans or checking again.

5

...

Motivating:
Respect, Money, and the
Little Things

People work to make money. It's called the bottom line, common wisdom that if the paycheck did not come regularly, there would be no one to do the work. It is an understanding that the money has to be available in order to have a work force in the first place.

However, studies and surveys indicate that people in the workplace have much more than money on their minds. While it is true that making a salary adequate to live on properly is motivation for virtually everybody, workers are also concerned about being treated well. They want their bosses to be fair and appreciate what they do. They not only want their efforts acknowledged, they want to be trusted that they are doing their best, that they can think for themselves, that their work is important to them. Very often, if the money is adequate but the other ingredients are not there, they will

go to a job that pays less money but offers more acknowledgment of their worth. The message is clear: As important
as money is, your most important motivating tool is showing
respect for those who work for you.

Showing respect for your workers in your role as
manager can take many forms. One of the particularly tricky
areas in this regard is the personal/professional boundary
line. Because the workplace provides such a social outlet,
questions about violating the line come up all the time. Where
does the boundary fall? How much does it depend on the
situation and particular people involved? Does it mean not
socializing at all? As impossible as general answers to these
questions are, there are things that every manager should
watch out for.

In the first place, don't think of yourself as a company
clone or as someone's soulmate. Neither extreme works.
Putting on a false front, answering the way you think a good
company person should answer, not being yourself, puts
co-workers off. Some managers feel it makes you more
efficient because you are not "wasting time" on emotional
connections. But any time gained is more than offset by the
distance between you and everyone else. People don't give
that extra effort for someone they don't care about.

On the other hand, don't expect people to confide in you.
You are not at work to listen to their personal problems or to
solve them. And understand that they don't want to listen to
your problems either. Assistants and secretaries are in a
particularly vulnerable position because of their lack of power
and their close working relationship to their boss. If you start
talking about personal problems such as the welfare of your
children or the state of your marriage, you have trespassed
the boundary line. An assistant will find it very uncomfortable
because she or he can't do anything about it, yet feels bound
to listen.

Below are some basic concerns workers have about being respected. They may seem little to you, but they mean a lot to those you work with:

- A personal touch is important. Although you should not play therapist, keeping completely closed off seems false because it's not the way we human beings operate. Taking a few minutes to ask about someone's spouse or vacation or new house shows them that you care about their lives.
- Say hello and good-bye when you come into the office and leave at night. People can feel very slighted by something as simple as your forgetting to do this. As one employee in a manufacturing plant aptly put it, "I want a boss to know I exist, that I'm not just another cockroach." And acknowledge people when you pass them in the halls; often just a smile or a nod will do fine.
- Understand that those you manage want to be excited about their work, no matter what level of the totem pole they're on. A secretary has as much pride in a well-typed document as a CEO does in a successful merger. If they want to take on more work, never say no; just make sure by careful follow-up that other duties will not be neglected for the new ones.
- Give credit. Nothing motivates like appreciation— especially in front of a third party. You give credit not only because you want to be fair, but because it's a tremendous morale booster. And remember that giving credit to someone who reports to you in no way takes away from your own accomplishments. It only strengthens your position as a good manager, someone perceived to have an eye for talent.

- Respect the decisions your subordinates make. Overturn these only if it's necessary, always explaining why you have had to do so.
- Realize the importance of "downtime." After you've been working hard on a particular project or have gone through a particularly hectic time, understand that everyone will need some breathing space. Slow the pace, relax the rules a little bit, perhaps have a lunch or a party.
- Don't keep people in the dark. You want to make those who work with you feel as though they are part of the company. Holding on to facts is often a way of saying that your co-workers don't count as much as you do. Be careful of this attitude. Share your view of the bigger picture, tell your employees the upshot of meetings, keep them informed of the company's goals and where it's headed.

Motivating the Mailroom

Any department composed of minimum-wage employees, such as a mailroom, will put special demands on your motivational abilities. These are the departments that don't get any respect, and yet when there are problems, the whole company comes running. Motivation is difficult because many—if not most—of the workers are only there for a paycheck. And people tend to undervalue such a department, thinking of it as the lowest on the totem pole, so consequently it is a department with which they often act condescending.

If you've been put in charge of a mailroom or a similar department, there are things you can do to make life easier for both yourself and your subordinates:

- Build self-respect as much as possible. Even the lowest-paying jobs carry pride of accomplishment. Always focus on this and point out the problems that develop when the job isn't well done.
- Roll with the punches. Employees in a mailroom are often street-smart kids. They are often good at teasing and testing. Learn to laugh with them.
- Be firm. Unfortunately, street-smart kids often have trouble with authority. Make it plain from day one that a proper attitude is expected of them, just as it is of all employees.
- Institute the best controls and checkpoints possible. Remind everyone that it's for their own good. Because of the volume of work that passes through, keeping track of everything is vital.
- If the situation warrants it, show them that you are on their side during disputes. Blaming the mailroom is corporate America's favorite pastime. If you've instituted good controls and the facts point to problems in other departments, make sure you support your workers. If they feel you're on their side, they'll work harder.
- Know how to tell the difference between excuses and real problems. Street-smart kids know how to give excuses: for being late, for being absent, for not doing a good job. Unfortunately, however, their life experiences are also often much more dramatic than your average manager has experienced. Learn to listen. The real problems are there, and you can tell in the animation, in the voice, in the details of the recounting. You will be able to feel that they are not giving you a story.

Money—the Bottom Line

And then we come to money. It is used to measure performance, being given as a reward for good work and being withheld when the work is bad. As such, it's regarded as the main tool of motivation by both workers and bosses. "You give me more money, and I'll do a better job" is the standard refrain. The problem is, sometimes the griping about money hides other things that may be bothering a worker. They may say it's about money when in reality it's about something else. This makes money a very touchy issue. A manager must learn to keep it in perspective, separating the personal from the monetary, the employee's desire for more money from the realities of the marketplace.

Not knowing what one can or cannot do in terms of giving a raise is one of the mistakes beginning managers make. When someone has done a particularly good job or complains that they are not being paid enough, many managers, in their haste to reward or appease someone, make promises that they cannot keep. Before you promise anyone anything, make sure you know how much money you are allowed to give someone. The personnel department or your boss will know. It's better to tell someone that you have to check with the powers that be before committing yourself than to come back later and apologetically say that you have to take back an offer.

Asking for a raise for someone is done through the hierarchy. In the first place, you should only do it if you honestly feel your employee deserves one. This will happen when they come to you, giving what you feel are valid reasons for the raise. You in turn go to your boss and present the reasons you were given. Also, compile a list of your own, pointing out specific areas where your employee shines. The more strongly you feel that the employee truly deserves the raise, the more persuasive you will be. Your boss may have an answer right away or may do his own checking, taking a few days to get back to you. Then you will report back to the person.

If you want to give someone a bonus to motivate them for a particularly difficult job, check with your boss first, get the okay, and then present it to the employee, pointing out that you did this because you know the job will be difficult and you expect their best effort. You can also save a bonus till the end as a special thank-you. In either case, point out that it is for *this particular job*. A bonus is exactly what the word means: something extra. The next time the employee is asked to do a similar project, you don't want them to automatically expect a bonus again.

Never discuss one employee's salary with another employee. It is a breach of confidence and can later cause you grief when someone complains about not getting equal remuneration to someone else. If two employees tell each other what they are making and one of them uses this as a way of trying to get more money, check their job descriptions, titles, experience, and performance reviews with the personnel department. Chances are that the person making more money is doing so for one of those reasons; if everything is truly equal you very well may have to equalize their pay.

The Pay Raise

Recommending pay raises for employees requires that you be clear about whether and how much of a raise someone deserves. Weigh the person's strength's and weaknesses, and especially their attitude in taking on work, correcting mistakes, and in general, trying to grow in their job. Compare the raises you've recommended for others who have done similar work. And be aware of the last raise you gave to this person, so this raise will not seem either too high or too low in comparison.

Giving a pay raise to an employee is a ritual you will be going through hundreds of times. Usually this is a pleasant experience; the employee has done a good job and you reward them with a raise. In discussing the raise, you should remember the following:

- Give the news to the person in your office; it's a formal occasion.
- Never belittle a raise, no matter how small it is. It's being given for a job well done and you should treat it as legitimate.
- If the raise is obviously average or smaller than the previous one, confront the issue head on. Whether it's because you don't think the employee did better-than-average work or whether it's due to company economics, tell the employee.
- Take note of the employee's response. If the person complains that the raise is too low and you don't think it is, put it in perspective. Point out that the salary is commensurate with the employee's responsibilities, position, and company guidelines. If the complaints seem persuasive, agree to check into the matter.
- Use the opportunity as a way of thanking the person, referring to a few things they have accomplished that you especially like. Also encourage them, urging them to continue doing well.

Turning Down a Request
For a Raise

Turning down a request for a raise is a little trickier, because you are saying no. In responding to such request, you should first be clear about why you don't think the person deserves more money. And have specific reasons and examples to back yourself up! Here are a few things to keep in mind when telling someone no.

- Be honest. Don't blame your boss or the company if you're the one who doesn't think a raise is deserved. The excuses will seem transparent. Also, this is the chance to voice your complaints and to try to improve things.
- If you really would like to get more money for the person but you know the company will not allow it, admit this also.
- Use the opportunity to set some goals, and agree to discuss the matter at some future date. But don't lead an employee on. Only do this if you think things might change for the better.
- Don't get into a bargaining situation. If you do, you are compromising your authority. Setting a future date leaves the door open, but it does not tie you down to any promises.
- Never say no in anger. If you feel that a request is particularly out of line, give yourself some time alone, cool down, collect your thoughts, and then call in the employee to give your reasons.

6

...

Working Together:
Know the Hierarchy

Any company is a hierarchy of people, some with more responsibility, others with less. This hierarchy is composed of people who influence the work of the company in various ways. You as manager have to understand how both the social aspect and the power structure play upon each other and influence your work. You have to know where you fit in. And how you can best use the people working for you, with you, and above you to do your job as manager

Underlining it all is the concept of authority that comes from setting boundaries. Everyone has their own "space"— both literally and figuratively—which must be respected. You don't step on toes and no one steps on yours, as the saying goes. Everyone knows their place and the job they are expected to do. No matter what level you're at, you as manager have a place too. And that place carries with it a certain level of authority.

Maintaining the level of authority—that fine line between you and everybody else—is part of your job as manager. It can sometimes be very difficult. On the one hand, you must respect the authority, the work, and the emotional needs of your co-workers. On the other hand, you will be making decisions every day that affect those very things. And they will be doing the same to you—from above and below. It means a constant shifting and testing of the boundaries, and it means always being sure where yours fall.

The issue of boundaries raises the question of having friends—is it okay? As far as a manager is concerned, he or she is no less human than anybody else. The thing to watch out for is that work and friendship don't take away from each other. This can happen in terms of time (too much time at work spent talking about non-work-related topics or too much time outside talking about work), information (letting a friend know confidential information), or proximity (working too closely with each other to want to spend social time together).

Being friends with those you manage directly will create problems if that friendship interferes with your authority. If you find yourself lowering your standards for someone who is a friend, being afraid to criticize their work too much, or showing favoritism in any other way, then it's time to reconsider your relationship. The closer you are to someone, the easier it is for such favoritism to develop. Human nature makes being one of the boys (or one of the girls) and still maintaining your authority an almost impossible task.

The issue of physical space is getting more and more attention these days. The bottom line is that it matters, not only in how good the lighting is or how big an office someone has, but in terms of boundaries as well. Use space to your advantage and understand how it pertains to you as manager.

- Don't invade personal space, even if you have authority over someone. You should never go through your assistant's desk. And don't hover around them.

- Understand that an office conveys power. Discussing something with your assistant in your office is very different from talking about it in the hall or by his desk. Just the act of calling an assistant into your office is an assertion of your authority.
- Your sitting behind a desk with someone else on the other side is the most formal, authoritative position you can take. If you want to make the person more at ease, provide seating side by side.
- Touch. Apart from any sexual innuendo, which is strictly taboo, touching someone at work brings up complex emotions. By and large it's not done, yet a hand on a shoulder or a hug when someone hears traumatic news and you don't know what to say is always appreciated. There is a wonderful line in *The One Minute Manager,* one of the most popular management books of recent years, in which authors Kenneth Blanchard and Spencer Johnson state that one should only use touch as a way of giving something, not taking. In that sense a touch will always be appreciated.

Your Assistant

In Chapter 1, a number of questions were given to help you clarify what you might expect from an assistant. This section will discuss how you as manager relate to your assistant in various situations, and how necessary it is to remain sensitive to their needs while maintaining that all-important fine line of authority.

A common problem to watch out for is the Perfect Assistant Syndrome. There is no such thing as a perfect assistant, yet many managers crave one all their professional lives. They are hiring and firing constantly, not from any particular mean-spiritedness, but because they truly believe they are not getting the help they deserve. They have to learn how to recognize their needs, which is why asking the questions in Chapter 1 is so important. You must decide on the qualities you want from your assistant and you must also accept the fact that everyone will have strengths and weaknesses.

Another insidious trap related to the Perfect Assistant Syndrome is to compare all subsequent assistants to one that was particularly outstanding. The biggest problem with this is that you often insist, without realizing it, that the other assistants do things the way the glorified assistant did them—precedents can be very strong in working life, just as they are in the legal system. You can end up overlooking the different strengths of another assistant because you are wedded to having certain things done in the old way. If you find yourself dissatisfied with something an assistant has done, ask yourself whether you are falling into that trap before you criticize or attempt to change the situation.

This brings up the problem of the new assistant. When the mistakes keep coming and the same questions and answers are repeated over and over, you may often wonder whether you have hired someone with adequate skills. How to judge and how much leeway to give? Time is the first indicator. Notice how long it takes the person to pick up particular skills. You can usually tell within the first week or two how quickly they are picking up routine tasks. But there is a difference between picking up routine tasks and being *comfortable* in a job. It can take a good assistant a few months to get all the basics down. As a way of gauging their progress, you can do the following things:

- Listen to the questions they are asking. Have they picked up any information at all or are the questions being asked in the same way?
- Attitude is very important. Does the person make an effort to correct mistakes immediately and stay late or come early to get on top of a particular problem?
- Does the person seem busy or bored? Is there a lost quality about them that indicates they are not in touch with the job?
- Look at yourself. You may be making things more difficult by throwing out new concepts and ideas in inappropriate or hostile ways. You may think you are teaching something, yet what you are really doing is making your assistant uncomfortable by pointing out what they still do not know.
- And make sure you are not comparing them to anyone—only to the requirements of the job.

Sometimes, due to a promotion or a new job, you find yourself with an inherited assistant—someone who worked for your predecessor and who will now be working for you. This is a difficult situation for both of you. The assistant has to realize that you may doing certain things differently from your predecessor, and that you have a right to do so. You have to realize that they have certain proprietary feelings because they have been doing that job longer than you have been managing them. They probably know a lot that you are not even aware of. Respect their knowledge and tap it, asking questions and admitting what you don't know. Integrate that information into your decisions, but remember that the decisions are now yours to make.

A word about grunt (i.e. dirty) work: That's what assistants are for, or so goes the common view. To a large degree that is the reality—copying, answering the phone, opening mail, doing any simple tasks—and you certainly can expect them to do these tasks. But if you think that's all your assistant can do, that's all that they will ever do, so don't forget about grunt work completely. Keep an eye on it and make a conscious effort to mix it up with more interesting tasks as a way of testing your assistant's skills and teaching them new ones.

Your Department

When you go from managing one person to several, everything becomes more complex. It is similar to a family, where a second child creates more than twice as many concerns as you had with one child: besides having another child to take care of, you now have to wonder how they will get along, whether you will have preferences for one or the other, how you will apportion your goods to meet their demands. It's a geometric progression of concerns, not a simple arithmetic one.

It is the same in managing a department, so much so that dealing with "people issues" can become your full-time job. In Chapter 4 we discussed the problems involved in assigning work. There are other issues to keep in mind as well:

- Make sure everyone's duties are spelled out clearly. The lines of authority are very important when people work together on a daily basis. Questions and problems to be resolved come up constantly.
- Know what's going on. You have to keep your finger in the pie as it were, because you are going to represent the department at various meetings and will be asked questions about the progress of work.

- Be aware of everyone's strengths and weaknesses and the job they do. You may not be able to do everyone's job as well as they can, but you should know its basics and how it acts upon the whole department.
- Be involved in everyone's job. Regularly scheduled meetings, one on one, are a good idea, both to inform yourself and to give feedback.
- Be careful of favoritism and of being drawn into various factions. Working together in close proximity magnifies everything. Jealousies and hurt feelings can spring up very easily in response to the smallest things you do.
- Have fun! Departments really are like families, both in their problems and in the close ties that develop. Birthday parties, promotion parties, surprise parties, impromptu get-togethers lessen tension and increase morale. Always make room for them and initiate them yourself.

Your Peers

Yes, you can manage your peers at the workplace, though you don't have authority over them. And you have a right to manage them. You work with them: asking for information, needing them to give you their work by a particular date so you can do the next step, coordinating various projects together. Managing without authority is a necessary management tool, a great skill to have, and wonderful training for the time when your authority will be increased.

Think of managing your peers as cooperation. It is the way you get them to do work while acknowledging their equal status in terms of the hierarchy. When conflicts develop, neither your concerns nor theirs take automatic precedence. You sit down to discuss these issues, giving right-of-way to whichever needs fit in more urgently with the bigger picture. Usually, you meet each other halfway. The following are important peer-management points:

- Show respect for their concerns. You may not know their job, but you should appreciate that it's equally important to yours. This attitude should color all your interactions with your peers.
- Make them respect your concerns. Be on top of your job—always—so that you have ready explanations for what you need. This also allows you to be clear and concise without taking up unnecessary time and annoying everyone.
- Be polite but persistent. If there are problems with something they owe you, you can't force them to do it. And losing your temper will just make things worse. On the other hand, don't be afraid to remind them.
- Only complain to the higher-ups if you've told them you would have to do so. Going behind someone's back creates ill will and mistrust. And the only way a higher-up can force them to do something is by acknowledging the problem and thereby tipping them off that you have complained.

Your Boss

The bottom line of managing your boss is that you should treat him or her the way you expect your assistant to treat you. You defer to your boss's authority, but you also know that you are valuable. And you want to make sure that your boss understands how valuable—not that you grab as much attention and credit as possible, but that you help a boss understand how your job helps them in their work. Here are the finer points of boss management:

- Keep your boss informed. Communication is important—nothing is more annoying to a boss than finding out about a problem before you have told her about it.
- Anticipate your boss's concerns. Keep an eye out for the things that matter to your boss, whether it's the way he likes information presented or how often he expects you to do certain things.
- Don't be a "yes-person". If you are overruled on something and you sincerely believe the decision is wrong, try to get it reversed. State your reasons for coming back and why they are important to you. Even if you are overruled again, you will only win respect for trying.
- Respond quickly to your boss's requests. They become a priority. Quick service is one of the perks of being a boss. If you feel you must do something else first, inform her. Then it becomes her responsibility to choose what you should do.
- Don't try to win favors from your boss or show how special you are. Concentrate on your job, and appreciation will take care of itself.
- You are not responsible for your boss's moods. His being in a bad mood might have nothing to do with you. A good boss will try to keep his moods from affecting his work, but if they do spill out over you occasionally, don't take it personally.

The Role of Personnel

The personnel or human resources department is underutilized by most managers. It is the one you see when you are first hired by a company, but often that is also the last time you make any real use of it. That is a shame because a good personnel department performs functions that are vital to every employee. You as manager should become familiar with it, remembering that it performs the following functions:

- It will answer questions you have about salaries, benefits, vacations, and health insurance. It is this department's job not only to maintain records pertaining to these things, but also to keep abreast of any development in these areas (for example, in new insurance that may be available).
- It is the front line in the hiring process. If you're new at your job of managing, a personnel department may understand better than you do what kind of person you need to fill a certain position. Talk to them about it. Remember, you can listen to their point of view, but in the end it's your decision.
- Use the personnel department if you are having problems with one of your co-workers, whether it's an assistant or a boss. Confidentiality is the rule. They've heard it before and can usually come up with solutions much less drastic than the ones you may be contemplating.

At bottom, a personnel department is there to watch out for every employee's self-esteem. If you're overwhelmed with the people issues you are dealing with, or need some things sorted out, the personnel department can put it all in better perspective.

7

···

Managing Problems:
Stay in Control

Sometimes it truly seems that all managers do is deal with problems: tension, fighting, inadequate systems, inadequate employees. And they feel responsible for it all. This chapter will examine some of the major problem areas and take a look at where a manager's responsibilities do fall.

Stress

Everything is late, coworkers are being uncooperative, the atmosphere is tense, schedules are impossible, and you find yourself

- constantly wanting to scream or yell
- secretly crying in the bathroom
- being angry at everybody
- always feeling overwhelmed

- sitting at your desk unable to move
- often sick
- never having time for a minute's socializing
- never laughing.

These are signs of stress—warnings that you are allowing the problems to get to you, indications that your emotions are in a precarious state.

Stressful situations are everywhere, and they don't go away. What you have to do is learn how to cope with them effectively, and the way you do that is to take control of stressful situations before they take control of you. This may sound impossible at first; you tell yourself that you are not creating the problems, you just somehow end up in the middle of them. But that is just the point. By allowing yourself to be in the middle, you are in effect creating the problems for yourself.

Suppose it's Tuesday morning and your grouch of a boss has just called, yelling at you for not turning in a report that was due this morning. You promise it to him ASAP, even though you have an important presentation to give tomorrow morning, for which you still have a lot of preparing to do. You also know that your assistant can't do the work for you. What do you do?

- First, take a minute: to think, to breathe, to stop everything. That is always the first step. Stopping for a moment acts like a circuit breaker and allows you to focus your energies, so that you do not succumb to the insanity around you.
- Identify what is bothering you the most. This means being very honest with yourself. In this situation you realize that all along you've known that the presentation was the more important of the two and that you

concentrated on it because you are tired of your boss's unreasonable expectations.

- Take responsibility. By realizing how you've prioritized your work, you've suddenly taken responsibility for what's happening to you. This takes away some of the feelings of powerlessness that fuel stress.
- Go through your options. You have to decide what to do next. That's a very important point to remember: Only you can relieve your own stress, no one can do it for you. And you always have choices. In this case you can stay up all night working, you can try to talk to your boss, you can call in sick tomorrow.
- Make your choice and then try to give the stress back. Suppose you decide—yet again—to be mature and talk to your unreasonable boss. You go in, apologize, tell the old coot how the presentation took over all your time, and propose giving him the report on Friday, which is as early as you think possible. If he agrees, that's great; even if he doesn't, you've given him some of the stress back by making him aware of the impossible demands he's putting on you.
- Accept the consequences. If your boss doesn't agree, you still have to accept the consequences. Now you make a further choice and decide to stay up all night. The cycle starts all over again. You take responsibility for being in this terrible situation and go through your options of how to avoid it in the future: you can plan your time better, you can anticipate your boss better, you can train your assistant more thoroughly, you can look for another job. That is how you control stress—by taking responsibility, by always focusing on your next step. Notice: There is a big difference between taking responsibility and taking blame. You never take blame. The situation is still terrible, your

boss is still unreasonable, but you—and only you!—
are doing something about it. It is basically changing
your attitude; but having this attitude is always a
great relief, and it brings results.

Procrastination

The above scenario also raises another issue: Why you feel
you haven't trained your assistant properly enough; why
you've been putting it off.

Procrastinating on something usually means you don't
want to do it because it's difficult (takes more of your
energies) or because you feel that you won't do it well
enough, so you don't even try. In the case of your assistant,
perhaps you feel that she is weak in certain areas of her job.
You haven't confronted the situation because confronting it
means you'll have to make the effort to train her; or; if she
just isn't good enough, you will have to decide whether to live
with it or get someone else. Neither is a pleasant prospect.

Procrastinating is also a bad use of time: You do the easy
things first, leaving the more difficult of unpleasant tasks till
the end of the day, when you suddenly find that it's time to go
home. Then you are stuck with either doing the difficult task
at night or carrying it over till the next day. And the next.
And the next. Always take the time to prioritize and do the
most important thing first.

In the case of those you manage, remember that they
are going through exactly the same fears and rationalizations
that you are. After you have decided to take action on your
own procrastination, find out why an assistant is putting
something off. Ask questions gently but firmly, and try to
remember what the result was when you gave them certain

jobs to do. They could be procrastinating for any of the following reasons:

- Anger. He could feel that it's not part of his job description. In that case you will have to talk it out and come to an understanding.
- Boredom. If she's not motivated, has she been in the job too long, are there other tasks to give her? Remember, however, that just like you, she will ultimately have to take responsibility for herself. There is only so much you can do.
- Fear. Something seems too complex or overwhelming in which case you can break it down into smaller parts. Or the fear may be due to other facts:

  - lack of certain skills. By questioning and trial and error you can find out what skills she lacks, and decide on how best she can acquire them
  - lack of experience. Even if she has the skills, if she's never done something before it can be very frightening
  - lack of talent. As opposed to skills, talent is deeper and more ingrained, involving personality, genes, likes and dislikes. You may just have to accept that someone is not talented in a particular area.

There is another frequently overlooked factor that may cause procrastination: things beyond your control. It is important to realize that this possibility exists, both for yourself and for your subordinates. In the case of your assistant, others may not be cooperating with her. She may or may not understand the extent of the problem—it will depend on how well she knows where her responsibilities end and those of others begin. This is where you can help out. Step in, point out where the responsibilities lie, and talk to co-workers, asking for their cooperation.

You may have the same problem yourself as you may be trying to accomplish something and yet feel blocked by lack of authority, uncooperative colleagues, and nonsupportive bosses. If you've tried the avenues of talking to them, asking for support or authority and still not getting it, it is time to swallow the disappointment and accept that something will just not get done.

Conflict

Because of the wide variety of tasks and the daily grind of getting things done, conflicts at the workplace are bound to occur. Whether you manage one person or several, you have to expect conflicts and know how to resolve them so that the work can proceed.

You may find yourself in a situation where your assistant is angry about something. In the first place, don't play his game. He may not be smiling or saying hello, but that does not mean you should act the same way. If nothing has been openly discussed, pretend everything is fine and wait for him to come talk to you to resolve the situation.

You shouldn't let brooding go on for too long, however. If you feel his anger shows no signs of abating, or is getting worse, you should broach the subject, saying you have noticed that he seems upset about something, and then wait for his response. He will usually tell you, and then you can go on to resolve the situation. If he still is not ready to talk, respect his privacy and do not try to pry it out of him. Your acknowledgment that you've noticed something is important in itself, and it will be easier for him to open up in the future.

Not prying into his anger assumes that his work has not been affected by his attitude. If it has, you have a right to point this out and ask for immediate improvement. This is also usually enough to start an honest exchange.

Sometimes the battle of wills is much more subtle. On the surface he seems the same, but he procrastinates. Or he says yes, but you can feel his heart isn't in it. In cases like this, note down a couple of examples and call him into your office to point them out. Don't act accusatory, just puzzled, which is what you are. You may find that he thinks things should be done differently or that you are not taking his views into account. He may be a bit confused himself and not sure what he wants. Your job is to make him relax and to ask questions to find out if there is legitimacy to what may be upsetting him.

By the same token, you may be angry at your assistant, in which case it is very tempting to give him the cold shoulder, look for extra work for him to do, or snap and lose your temper. All of these reactions are game playing and power plays. They are not in your best interests because you just make a bad situation worse. Be honest with yourself and admit why you're angry. If it's something petty, forget it; if it's legitimate, sit down and talk to him. You can admit your anger without losing your temper. And if he finds the courage to talk to you first, never put him off. You should feel grateful that he is trying to improve something that is more your problem than his.

After any period of bad feelings or tense exchanges, it's always good to have an everything-is-back-to-normal conversation. Basically, it means operating the way you did before, perhaps talking about an aspect of work that is going well, or mentioning something about a non-work-related topic that you both enjoy, or throwing out a funny line and making a joke at your own expense.

When you are running a department, conflicts usually arise when your subordinates bicker over work. Someone is jealous of someone else's projects, another person feels she is doing too much. There are also clashes over titles and authority, and personality clashes where two people simply rub each other the wrong way. Your job as manager is not to get in the middle of it, but to

- make sure all lines of responsibility are clear
- watch out for favoritism
- stay out of personal conflicts
- always insist that work is the priority, not personalities
- learn how to listen between the lines—in conflict situations people either overdramatize or tell half-truths to support their point of view, so hone your listening skills
- avoid discussing one person's work with another—unless they are both present to resolve a particular issue

You certainly can tailor your responses to specific conflicts. For example, give out assignments so that two people whose personalities clash will be working together as little as possible. However, if the situation is unavoidable, you have to remember that the work comes first; they have to learn to work through their differences.

Emotional Problems/Substance Abuse

You may be faced with a situation in which an employee is coping with serious emotional problems or substance abuse. The most important thing to remember about such a situation is that you should not become involved in the problem itself. You are the person's boss, not a therapist, and while you always want to treat them as humanely as possible, your main concern is their work performance.

Work performance is your basic tool for gauging that something is going wrong. If a previously competent employee shows a marked deterioration in how well he or she performs tasks—accuracy, enthusiasm, volume of work are all indicators—that may be a sign that deeper problems are involved. There are other indications as well: a person's basic energy level goes down; they are moody; their appearance becomes disheveled; they remain sullen or expressionless throughout most of the day; they disappear for long periods of time without informing you; everything seems a struggle; they are often sick, absent, or late. Once you have noticed any or all of these changes, you as manager need to act:

- Confront the person. Tell them you have noticed that something seems awry, without accusing or second-guessing or jumping to any conclusions. Wait for their response. They may agree with you, they may not.
- Say that you can't tolerate the situation. Even if they don't agree with you and take the position that their personal life is not your concern, you must emphasize that their work is. Give specific examples of where the work has gone down. Make it clear that if the situation continues or gets worse, you will have to let the person go.
- Guide them to get help. *Guide* is the operative word. Initially, you may listen if they open up and tell you what is bothering them. After all, you do care about them. But you do not become a confessor or a problem solver. Tell them how concerned you are

that they get help and guide them to any particular programs or groups that may be available in your area. Make yourself cognizant of them; check with your personnel department. Your employee is valuable to you, and you want to give them the best chance possible for solving their problem and continuing to do a good job for you.

If you have tried the solutions mentioned above, and things are still not working out, you have to start seriously considering firing the person. Asking someone to leave because of budgetary problems or staff cuts is also a possibility, and in that case firing is usually referred to as "laying someone off." Although the reasons are different, many of the concerns and procedures you follow are the same.

The process is composed of three stages: your preparation for the firing, the actual firing, and dealing with the aftermath. Each has specific requirements.

Firing: The Preparation

Before you even think of firing someone, there are certain things you should make sure you have been doing correctly. They are important to protect your company from lawsuits or more unpleasantness than is necessary. Essentially, they have to do with your treatment of all the people you manage—not only the person in question. Your main concern is consistency—everybody follows the same rules, gets the same reprimands and rewards. You want to be fair so that no one can say you are getting rid of someone for reasons other than job performance.

In situations like this it is good to be conscious of

standards: your own and the company's. What do you expect in this job, why is this particular person falling short, to what degree have you accepted lower standards in the past? This is also why a job description is so important. Someone may claim that they are not doing something because it's not in their job description, or that the job was misrepresented. Be aware of whether the job description has changed and if so, why. What were other employees in that same position expected to do? You don't want to seem as though you are fluctuating from one person to the next.

Also, be careful of what you may have promised someone, especially if it's in writing. If you've reneged on a job promise, make sure you can back yourself up with good reasons. It doesn't mean you should be afraid to say no; it means you don't do things arbitrarily.

Below is a list of reasons why you can fire someone:

- incompetence
- bad attitude (talking back to you; not trying)
- chronic lateness
- chronic absenteeism
- gross misconduct (cheating, stealing, fighting: someone can be fired after one such violation)

Reasons why you cannot fire someone:

- age
- sex
- religious affiliation
- ethnic status
- salary (you can't fire someone simply because they are now making too much money)
- someone's behavior away from the job that may have come to your attention (though if there are problems away from work, there are often problems at work also)

When you are preparing to fire someone, you also have to make sure that the disciplinary process has been fair and reasonable. This is not only for the employee's protection, but for yours also. For this reason, it is important to make some notes when problems occur so that you have specifics handy should they ever be needed when talking to your subordinate or when answering the questions of personnel and your own bosses. Ideally, when you first started seriously considering that someone may not be working out, you already had some things written down.

The most important factor in the disciplinary process itself is to make sure that you have given the employee adequate warnings and chances to improve. That is why regular feedback is so important: nothing should come out of the blue. Verbal warnings are your first step; they are more informal and less threatening. If they aren't working, write up a formal report or memo, which goes to the personnel department, and which your employee has a right to see and respond to. Some managers use the official performance reviews for this purpose, though if the timing isn't right you shouldn't wait six months or a year before making an official complaint.

It's always a good idea—for your own peace of mind and your employee's information—to have a last-chance warning. Your employee will know where they stand, and it will give you a definite starting point for what is sure to be an unpleasant process.

Firing: Breaking the News

Firing someone is done at a formal meeting in your office. It is preplanned. You never fire someone off the cuff, out of anger, or as the mood strikes you. It is a rational decision.

As far as whether you fire on a Friday or a Monday, or before someone's vacation or after, there are no rules—it all depends on circumstances. Considering how high up the person is and how well you trust them, you may want to give them a few working days to clean out their office, get their paperwork in order, and inform any business contacts should they wish to do so. Worrying about ruining someone's weekend should not be a concern. As far as vacations go, most managers feel that firing someone after a vacation is more humane. The same holds true for end-of-year firings, where you wait till the new year to allow the person to accrue any yearly benefits that may be coming to them.

The following are the factors you should keep in mind about the meeting itself:

- Be in control of your emotions. Planning is important, because chances are you're still angry or frustrated or both. Yet you can't let your feelings guide what you say, any more than you let them guide your decision in the first place. Planning allows time for thinking it through and putting those feelings in the background.
- Never be rude or insulting. Number one: You don't want to rub salt in someone's wounds. Number two: It can be used against you.
- Don't be ambiguous. Some managers are so afraid of hurting someone's feelings that the person being fired is confused as to whether it's really happening.
- Make the meeting as short as possible. Be clear and succinct so you don't prolong their suffering, or yours.

The person being fired can have different reactions to the news, all of which you will have to be prepared for:

- Rage. Never respond to temper tantrums with anger of your own. Listen quietly to whatever they have to say and then finish what you have to say. If you are afraid that they may become irrational or threaten violence, stop the meeting at once.

- Crying. Be sympathetic, acknowledge how difficult it is for them, but don't back down. And don't be patronizing, saying it hurts you more than them, etc. It's still harder for them than it is for you.

- Silence. A mild-mannered person may be so flustered, he or she may sit quietly without seeming to have any reaction. Ask questions to make sure that they understand what is happening and why.

Listen carefully to what the person has to say, no matter how they react. Although the disciplinary process should have allowed for them to respond to your warnings, sometimes the heightened drama of the moment causes someone to blurt out new insights or confessions. At this stage you can't let these statements change your mind, but you can learn something and perhaps make it all a little less painful.

And remember, although letting someone go because of budget cuts or staff layoffs is still very difficult (after all, why didn't you choose someone else to lay off?), at least you are not directly criticizing the person's performance. In this case, it is much easier (and more truthful) to be genuinely positive, praising the good work the person has done and saying how sorry you are that things have come to such an undesirable state.

Firing: The Aftermath

The general rule for how quickly someone should leave the place of work after he or she has been fired is, the quicker the better. They certainly don't want to stay around, and you don't want them to, either. No matter how amicable the actual meeting might have been, there will be some tension between the two of you. Let them go. They do not owe you any work once they've been fired.

As stated earlier, depending on someone's position in the hierarchy, you may wish to give them a few days to clean up. Propose this at the meeting: for example, requesting that a person leave by Friday if they are being fired on a Monday. Some people will take you up on it, others won't. If you do give them a few days, however, you have to be prepared for the added stress that continued contact will bring. They also may be angry enough to stir up other co-workers, either by complaining about how unfairly they have been treated or by informing others what a bad manager you are. Be prepared for these possibilities.

You should also give yourself time to recover. Take some time after the meeting to wind down or talk to a trusted associate. Some managers feel they recover best if they go right back to work. That's fine and good, but you have to remember the stress you've just been under. If you can avoid it, don't work on a project where a bad decision may have crucial repercussions, or where you might start snapping at other employees. At a time like this it is best to do routine busywork that is not so taxing.

You will probably discuss the firing with your own boss or the personnel director. Draw the line there. The firing is a private matter between you and the person just let go. You owe them that courtesy.

You also have to remember that you are now responsible for that person's work. You have to figure out how much of it can be set aside. If you have others working for you, you have to decide how you will apportion what can't wait. That is another reason for good planning: you do not want to be left stuck in the middle of a big project or some other task that the person who was fired was doing for you.